A Great Idea

The Nexi Robot

by Toney Allman

NORWOOD HOUSE PRESS

Norwood House Press
P.O. Box 316598
Chicago, Illinois 60631

For information regarding Norwood House Press, please visit our Web site at:

www.norwoodhousepress.com or call 866-565-2900.

PHOTO CREDITS: Cover: © Mike Lee/VisualLee Photography; AFP/Getty Images, 22; AP Images, 27, 35, 37, 39, 40, 41, 42; © George Steinmetz/CORBIS, 10, 14; Getty Images, 7, 33; Haruyoshi Yamaguchi/Bloomberg News/Landov, 11; © Karel Lorier/Alamy, 15; © Mike Lee/VisualLee Photography, 17, 18, 19, 21, 13, 24, 26, 29, 30; Robert Gilhooly/Bloomberg News/Landov, 5; © Rick Friedman/CORBIS, 9; Wolfgang Thieme.dpa/Landov, 6; Yuriko Nakao/Reuters/Landov, 16

LIBRARY OF CONGRESS CATALOGING-IN-PUBLICATION DATA

Allman, Toney.
  The Nexi robot / Toney Allman.
    p. cm. — (A great idea)
  Includes bibliographical references and index.
  Summary: "Nexi is one of a team of four small humanoid robots that have mobility, dexterity and 'social' communication skills"—Provided by publisher.
    ISBN-13: 978-1-59953-342-1 (library edition: alk. paper)
    ISBN-10: 1-59953-342-1 (library edition: alk. paper)
  1. Robots—Juvenile literature. 2. Androids—Juvenile literature. 3. Personal robotics—Juvenile literature. I. Title.
  TJ211.2.A464 2009
  629.8'92—dc22
                                                                    2009014714

Manufactured in the United States of America in North Mankato, Minnesota.
153R-022010

Contents

Note: Words that are **bolded** in the text are defined in the glossary on page 44.

Chapter 1

The Century of the Robot

Growing Up to Robotics

Cynthia Breazeal was born in 1967 in New Mexico. She spent her childhood in Livermore, California. She was a girl who loved sports, but she enjoyed science, too. Both of her parents were scientists. When she was in high school, she wanted to be a doctor. Then she went to college at the University of California at Santa Barbara. At college, she decided she wanted to work for NASA (National Aeronautics and Space Administration) and be an astronaut. She studied computer science and electrical engineering. Then she learned about the robots NASA was building. They would be rovers that explored the moon and planets. This seemed so exciting that she changed her mind again. She wanted to learn how to build robots. She decided to go to MIT for graduate school. There, her first robot work as a student involved designing tiny robot rovers for space exploration.

Cynthia Breazeal was 10 years old in 1977. She went to see the movie *Star Wars*. Her favorite part about the movie was the robots. She fell in love with them. She loved their personalities and their emotions. They had relationships with each other, and they interacted with people. She thought they were like friends, instead of just tools to use. She saw that the robots seemed to care about one another. They seemed to care about their people friends, too. Young Cynthia wanted to meet robots like those *Star Wars* robots. She wanted them to be real.

Robots of Today

Robots are real but, for now, they are still only tools. Many scientists say that the 21st century is the century of robots. Robots are found in many places and do many kinds of jobs. Scientists estimate that about 1 million robots are working in the world today. They help people in lots of ways. But they do not communicate like people do. They are devices that can do complex jobs. They do not look like people or animals either.

In modern factories, for example, robots do much of the work. A robotic arm

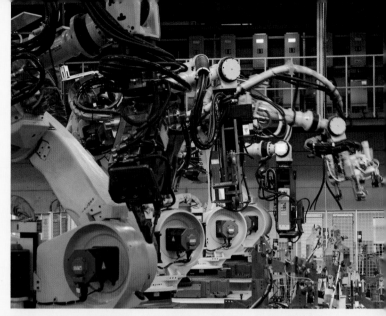

Robots have taken over many of the tasks that humans once did. In this Nissan auto factory, robots weld car parts together.

may weld two metal pieces together. The welding tool is built right into the robotic arm. A different kind of arm is called a pick-and-place robot. It may pick up a product off a **conveyor belt** and place it in a packing box. Pick-and-place robots are also used to build computers. They

An employee at a Nissan factory programs a robotic arm. Robots can operate small parts with better precision than humans.

can pick up very tiny electronic parts and then put them in the right place on computer circuit boards.

These special arms are **programmed** to do their jobs. They are only arms, but they are still robots. They are mechanical devices that are built to do jobs that people used to do. The jobs are either too dirty, too boring, or too hard for people. Robotic arms are programmed like computers to do these jobs. They are carefully built to be able to move, bend, and grasp without any human help. They may run on a battery or electricity. With the right power, they can be turned on and set to work.

At Work Everywhere

Another kind of robot vacuums people's floors. It is called the Roomba. By itself, it cleans floors and then parks in its base when it is finished. It can signal its owner with beeps if it gets stuck. It can even tell how dirty a floor is. When it finds a lot of dirt, it works on that spot over and over until the dirt is gone. Roomba operates

without human control. It is a robot that uses battery power, has a round body built to do a job, and a program.

Scientists use very complex robots in space and under the sea. On Mars, two robots named Spirit and Opportunity are exploring the planet. They follow instructions from people on Earth. They drive around the landscape, use tools to get samples of Mars, and test the chemicals found in Martian rocks and soil. They look at Mars with their camera eyes and send the pictures back to the scientists.

On Earth, other robots explore the deep ocean. They make maps of the ocean floor and collect samples of sea life. Still other

A Roomba, a robotic vacuum, can sense a room's size and is able to avoid bumping into furniture while it cleans.

robots hunt for explosive mines. These may be found in the ocean or on land. The robots can find dangerous mines and safely disarm them.

All of these robots are amazing. They can perform very complicated tasks and seem very smart. But these robots are not **social**. They do not have personalities. They cannot **interact** with people. They do not talk with people. They do not relate to people. Scientists have to program them to do what they do. They are not friendly beings like movie robots. Breazeal wanted to change all of that.

A Different Robot Idea

Breazeal wanted to develop robots that interact with people, not things. When she grew up, she decided to study **robotics**. She went to the Massachusetts Institute of Technology (MIT) in Boston. In 1990 she worked with her teacher, Professor Rodney Brooks, in his Humanoid Robotics Lab. Brooks decided to try to build a humanoid robot. Breazeal worked with

Did You Know?

Every year since 1997, teams of robots designed by university students around the world play soccer against each other in the RoboCup World Championship. In 2008 the competition was held in Suzhou, China. In the four-legged division, the German university team of Sony Aibo robots beat the Australians for the championship by a score of 5 to 0.

The First American Robot

Half of the robots in the United States are used in the car industry. Most are robotic arms that lift heavy parts, paint cars, and weld parts together. Joseph Engelberger is the father of American factory robots. He built the first one. It was named Unimate and was a robotic arm. In 1961 Unimate went to work at a General Motors factory. Unimate worked for fifty years before it was retired and sent to the Smithsonian Institution in Washington, D.C. The museum displays Unimate as an important first in American history.

Professor Rodney Brooks, director of the humanoid robotic group at the Massachusetts Institute of Technology, led the team that designed Cog. Cynthia Breazeal was a member of the team.

her teacher. They studied how to build robots that are like humans. This meant learning to program a robot in a completely different way. The robot would not have a specific job to do. Instead, it would have the job of learning to do new things. It would have to learn from people. It would interact with people and learn from its **environment**. It would learn with its senses—sight, hearing, and touching with its hands. It would learn by **imitating** what it was shown.

Cog

Breazeal and Brooks wanted to invent a robot as smart as a little child. They wanted a robot that could learn how to learn. Children learn by using their bodies to interact with the world. A robot that could learn would have to be built that way, too. Together, the scientists built a robot named Cog. Cog did not have legs and could not walk. It was a metal body with arms, hands, a neck, and a head. It did not have a real face. Its brain was a network of computers. Its job was to learn how to learn. It used its body and senses to do this. It had video cameras for eyes. It had microphones for ears. It had a voice and could say a few words. The eyes were programmed to learn how to watch things. Cog learned to use its eyes to follow people as they moved

Rodney Brooks (left) and a student help Cog the robot learn to play with Slinky toys in the lab. Cog learned by imitation.

around the room. Cog was programmed to turn its head to look at toys, too. It had to learn how to look at and then aim for a toy with its "hands," just like a baby. After 2,000 tries, the robot learned to grasp a toy that it saw.

Next, they taught Cog how to play with a toy. They handed Cog a Slinky. They showed Cog how to play with it by moving it back and forth between its two hands. Cog learned to do this after a few hours of practice. It was imitating what it was shown. It also learned to imitate play with a ball and a drumstick. Cog learned from experience, just like little children do.

Cog was an exciting robot because it could imitate and learn. But it was not social, and it could not build on what it

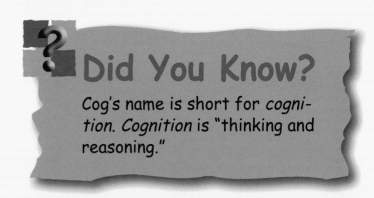

learned. Simple imitation was as far as it could go. One day, Breazeal put an eraser in front of Cog. Cog picked it up. Then Cog set it down again. Breazeal picked it up and put it down. Cog did the same. It looked like a game, but Breazeal knew it was not. The robot had learned to imitate, but it was not social. It was not interacting with her in a friendly way. It was not having fun with the game. It did not "want" to play. Cog was only a little bit like a child. To be a social robot, it had to have many more skills.

Friend or Foe?

Many Americans do not like the idea of teachable, social robots. They worry that the robots will get too smart. Perhaps the robots will somehow begin to stop taking human commands and begin to do things on their own. In Japan, people tend to look at robots in a different way. They see robots as gentle and friendly. They like the idea of robots. Maybe that is why Japan already has more robots than the United States has. The United States has 68 factory robots for every 10,000 people. Japan has 329 robots for every 10,000 people. Every year, the robots get more complex.

Many Japanese view robots as friendly helpers, whereas many Americans are more suspicious of them.

The First Step to a Social Robot

Breazeal decided to learn to build truly social robots. This meant that she would have to learn to program many different kinds of social skills. And she would have to learn to program these skills, one at a time, in different kinds of robots. Then, perhaps, she could build a social robot with a real personality.

Chapter 2

Robots with Personality

Cynthia Breazeal is a professor now. She is the head of the Personal Robots Group at MIT. She and her students are a robotics team. They are working to develop social robots. Programming social robots is very complicated. Other robotic teams are helping them. Some former MIT students started a robot company named Xitome. They are helping Dr. Breazeal's team build the robots. Another team of scientists at the University of Massachusetts at Amherst joined the effort, too. Altogether, these teams are programming robots to interact with people instead of things. Breazeal explains that they want to see if they can build robots that are not just tools.

Kismet

In 2000, while she was still a student, Cynthia Breazeal built the world's first social robot. It was a robotic head named Kismet. Kismet had two large eyeballs that could watch people. Breazeal bought big false eyelashes and glued them over the robot's eyes. Kismet also had furry eyebrows. Its mouth had rubber tubing for lips. Breazeal colored the lips with a red pen. Kismet could hear when a person spoke into a microphone. Kismet was programmed to act like a baby. Fifteen computers ran its programs.

Kismet had three skills. It was social because it babbled like a baby when people spoke to it. Second, it had a drive to learn about the world, like a baby does. When it was "bored" it looked at toys in the distance. Then people would bring it the toy and hold the toy up to its eyes. Finally, when Kismet had enough interaction, it was programmed to be tired. It would look away

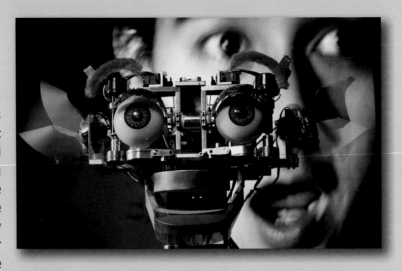

Kismet, a social robot created by Cynthia Breazeal, had an appealing, friendly face. Kismet was designed to imitate a baby learning about its world.

and stop babbling and looking at things. Kismet also could frown and look surprised by raising and lowering its eyebrows. This made the robot seem a little bit emotional. Kismet could not learn or remember, but it was a big step for robotics. It was a new kind of robot—not built to do a job, but built to react to its environment.

What Makes a Robot Social?

Dr. Breazeal's team has two major goals. First, they want to know what would make people enjoy robots. If people do not like a robot, they will not want to be around it. They will not interact with it or teach it things. So making a likable robot is very important.

The other major goal is to program a robot that can interact with people. That would make it a social robot. A social robot has to have two important features. It must have a body so it can interact with the world, and it must be able to sense and respond to its environment. No tool can do this. The robot would have to be programmed to have senses. And it would have to be programmed to learn how to learn from people. It would have to understand people and their emotions and behavior.

A mother plays on the floor with her baby. Scientists who design social robots are inspired by how infants learn.

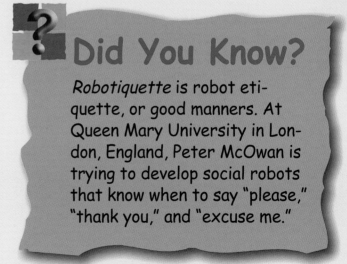

Did You Know?

Robotiquette is robot etiquette, or good manners. At Queen Mary University in London, England, Peter McOwan is trying to develop social robots that know when to say "please," "thank you," and "excuse me."

New Programs for New Robots

Dr. Breazeal decided that people like robots that seem social. She studied how babies learn because babies are social. They do not know very much, but adults like to be with them. Babies learn with their senses. They learn by moving their bodies. They learn by imitating people. They learn with curiosity and practice. They learn by interacting with other people. Breazeal figured that social robots would have to learn the same way. But all these social skills are very hard to program. Breazeal's team had to program robots in a whole new way. They took it step by step. They developed several robots that could do some personal, social things.

Kansei

Kansei is an emotional robotic head from Japan. (*Kansei* means "emotional" in Japanese.) Its face is a flexible, rubbery mask that can make different expressions. It is programmed to show emotions in response to words. For example, if it hears a "bad" word like *bomb* or *war*, it makes a scared or sad face. If it hears a "good" word like *toy* or *sushi*, it makes a happy face. The robot does not decide whether to like a word or not. Its responses to 500,000 words are already programmed into it by scientists.

Kansei the Japanese robot displays fear as it responds to certain programmed key words.

Helpful, Watching Eyes

AUR does not look like a social robot. It looks like a robotic arm. It is a desk lamp. But AUR can do something social. It can respond to the person using it. It is programmed to watch where a person is moving and what he or she is doing. Then, it shines its light where the person needs it. It can also sense how dark the person's workspace is. If more light is needed, it makes itself brighter. When the person leaves his or her desk, AUR turns itself off. AUR has one social skill. It uses a sense (an eye) to follow its user's movements. Then it changes what it does because of what it "sees."

Sensing the Environment

Huggable has more senses than AUR. It seems more likable and friendly, too. It is a cute, cuddly teddy bear. It has eyes, a sense of touch, microphones for ears, and a speaker for talking. It is programmed with 1,500 ways to sense the world. Most of these sensors are in its "skin."

Some robots are built to appeal to children, like the cuddly teddy bear interactive robot, Huggable.

Huggable is not exactly a robot because it does not act on its own. It is called an interactive teddy bear. It is built so that a far-away person can use it to interact with its owner. For example, a grandmother could interact with a young child who owned the bear. Through a computer, the grandmother could relate to the child by knowing what Huggable sees, hears, and feels. This would keep her in touch with her grandchild. She could tell the child a story through the teddy bear. She could make it laugh when the child tickled it. She could make the bear give the child a hug. Breazeal and her team call interacting through a robot "**puppeteering**." The robot is similar to a puppet operated by remote control. Huggable has a body and senses, but it is not social unless someone operates it.

Stripped of its furry, cute exterior, Huggable is a bundle of complex circuits and wires.

Interacting with a Person

Autom is a robot that does not need a remote control. It does not have a body. It is a plastic head on top of a computer chest with a touch screen. It has two eyes, but its only sense is a camera that watches its owner. It is a social robot programmed to do one job. It helps people lose weight. Autom speaks friendly greetings. It asks the person to enter his or her weight-loss goals on the computer. Every day, it asks the person to enter what foods he or she ate. It asks about exercise, too. Team member Cory Kidd developed Autom. In an interview on ABC television's *Good Morning America,* Kidd explained how it works. He said, "Autom is a weight-loss coach. So what she does is talk to you about how much you're eating and exercising."

Autom the interactive robot has progressed from helping people lose weight to working as a "roboceptionist."

Autom looks at a person with its eyes. It sounds happy when the dieter meets his or her goals. It sounds sad when the dieter ate too much. Robin Marantz Henig is a writer for the *New York Times*. She went to the lab to learn about Autom.

She reported that it says out loud, "You should congratulate yourself on meeting your calorie goals today." Or it may say, "It looks like you've had a little more to eat than usual recently." People who have used Autom say it is likable and fun. Autom is simple enough that it can be used by ordinary people in their homes.

Did You Know?

Cynthia Breazeal's team designed a garden of robot flowers. The flowers light up, bend, sway, ripple, and glow when a person comes near them. They are programmed to sense the warmth of a nearby human hand.

Interacting and Learning to Learn

Autom can interact with people about diets, but it can be social only in this one way. Leonardo can do much more. Leonardo, or Leo for short, is a very social robot. It looks like a furry little creature. It seems childlike and playful. Although it cannot walk, it does have a creature's body, with arms and legs. Its face can make many different expressions. It uses its eyes to look at people and remember them. It remembers their names, too. A student in the lab can ask Leo to find a certain person by name, and Leo will look right at that person because it has remembered him or her.

Leo can learn from people. It is programmed to recognize people's emotions. For example, a team member

Leonardo sits in the lab at MIT. Leo is so complex that it takes several computers to operate it.

named Mattie acted excited and happy to see a Big Bird toy. This made Leo reach for the toy. Leo acted like it wanted Big Bird for itself. Then Mattie pretended to be scared of Cookie Monster. Leo noticed Mattie's expressions and bad tone of voice. Leo turned away and would not hold that toy.

Leo is programmed to mimic people, too. It can imitate people doing puzzles. It can explore toys the way that Cog did. When Leo does not understand what to do, it shrugs its shoulders. Leo seems to learn the way children do. However, it is so complicated that it is run by a whole system of computers in the MIT lab. It can interact only with scientists who know how to teach it.

Can You Feel This?

Japanese scientist Takayasu Sakurai has designed robot skin. It is a flexible material embedded with transistors. It makes a robot's skin sensitive to pressure and heat. This is like having the sense of touch. A sense of touch is especially important for robot fingers. The fingers can gently pick up an egg without crushing the shell. They can shake a person's hand without too much pressure. Having good skin will be important for robots of the future. It will make them able to function in everyday life. Someday, robot bodies may all be covered with Sakurai's robot skin.

A scientist at Tokyo University holds up sophisticated and flexible robot skin next to a robotic hand.

Time to Put It All Together

Leo is an amazing robot, but it is just one more step on the journey to building a social robot for use in the real world. In 2008 Breazeal and her team felt ready to build a complete robot that combined the skills of Leo and the other robots. It would be an MDS robot—mobile/**dexterous**/social. It would be able to move around, use its body and hands in the environment, and act sociably and friendly. It would be a prototype—a first example—of the personal robots of the future. It would be the Nexi robot.

Chapter 3

Nexi, the Social Robot

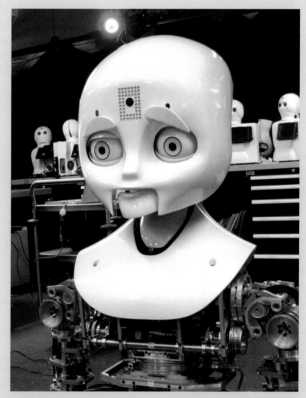

Nexi the robot awaits completion in the MIT lab. Nexi is child-sized to make interaction with humans easier.

Nexi is the latest amazing robot from Breazeal's team. It is so complex that different groups of team members had to develop its different parts. Some team members built its body. Other team members worked on its head. Others gave Nexi its hands. Still others programmed it to learn and interact with people. Nexi had to have lots of skills to be a complete MDS robot. In 2008 they were finally ready to show Nexi off to the world.

Cute and Capable Nexi

Nexi is built to be the size of a small child. Breazeal says that small robots fit better into people's lives. She also thinks that people will interact best with a child-sized robot. They could make friends with it and teach it. So Nexi is just three feet (1m) tall. It is shaped like a real person, but it looks more like a puppet or a cartoon. Its head, chest, and body are molded in plastic. The plastic fits over its metal and computer insides. Nexi's head has a face and sits on a movable neck. The face has eyes, a mouth, and the shape of a nose. Nexi has a body, but it does not have legs. Instead it uses wheels to be mobile. It is a bit easier to program moving on wheels than walking on legs. The wheels are like the wheels of a Segway scooter. This helps Nexi to balance

Using wheels instead of robot legs allows Nexi to move more smoothly, avoiding jerky leg movements.

as it rolls around. On its wheels, Nexi can travel about as fast as a walking person.

Nexi has two arms with very dexterous hands. It also has the sense of touch. The hands have wrists that can move and bend like a person's wrists. On each hand are a thumb and three fingers. With these hands and fingers, Nexi can lift an object that weighs up to 10 pounds (4.5kg). It can pick up small objects, too, and explore them with its sense of touch. Nexi can even gesture with its hands. It raises and waves its arms and opens its hands as it interacts with a person.

Sensing the World

Nexi also has complex senses. When it moves, it is programmed to make a map of its environment. It does not bump into

Nexi's Power

Nexi is powered with special lithium-ion batteries. The charge in the batteries lasts only about 45 minutes. Then the batteries have to be recharged. This short battery life is one reason that Nexi is not yet ready for the real world. To be practical outside the lab, a robot would need to run for at least several hours at a time.

things or get stuck. It recognizes objects and furniture in a room. It does this with a special camera in its forehead. It has other cameras that "see" for its two eyes. The eyes are blue and have dark pupils at the center. They can move, too, just like a person's eyes. Nexi can recognize people and follow them with its eyes as they move around a room. When a person speaks

Cynthia Breazeal shows Nexi to a group of students. Breazeal, standing, maneuvers the robot on the lab floor.

? Did You Know?

Nexi was chosen as number 17 in *Time* magazine's 50 "Best Inventions of 2008."

to the robot, Nexi knows to look at that person and pay attention. Nexi's "ears" are four special microphones. The microphones let Nexi know from which direction a sound is coming. It turns and looks at the sound or the person speaking. Nexi has another microphone and a speaker for its own voice. It has a woman's voice, and the voice is pleasant and has expression.

The Emotional Robot

Nexi has skills that most robots do not have. Its senses, **dexterity**, and mobility are amazing. But most important, it is social. It can show emotions on its face. Nexi has plastic eyebrows that move, eyelids that blink, and a jaw that moves its mouth and lips. It bends its neck in different ways and can nod or shake its

ASIMO

The Honda Corporation says that its ASIMO robots are the most advanced humanoid robots in the world. By 2009 Honda had built more than 100 ASIMOs. The ASIMO robot is not built to be social but to be smart and independent. The robot's name stands for Advanced Step in **Innovative** Mobility. ASIMO looks like a person in a space suit. It has a blank helmet window instead of a face. It walks easily on its two legs and can even run. It walks around doing jobs while sensing and not running into people and objects in the room. It can carry a tray or push a food cart with its hands and arms. It helps people by serving food and drinks to them, like a waiter. It can hear and respond to orders from people and follow directions. It understands waving, pointing at objects, and shaking hands. It knows its name and turns to face the person who calls its name. It also can recognize and remember about ten

Honda Motor Company demonstrates its newest ASIMO humanoid robots.

people by name and face. It can go to its base and recharge when it is running low on battery power. In many ways, ASIMO is more advanced than Nexi, but it does not show emotions. It is not programmed to learn like a baby. Instead, it is programmed to accomplish a variety of complex jobs.

head. It moves its facial parts in ways that show people different feelings. People who meet Nexi instantly recognize the emotion on its face.

Nexi can raise its eyebrows and open its mouth wide in surprise. The eyebrows can turn in and frown, too. Nexi's eyelids make slits over staring eyes to look mad. Its mouth turns down for sadness and up for happiness. Its eyes cast down or look to the side for sad or confused emotions. They open wide when Nexi seems excited or is paying attention to something. Other combinations of movements of eyelids, mouth, and eyes make Nexi look worried or shy. In an official video posted on You-Tube by the Personal Robots Group, Nexi explains, "I can tell you that I'm sad, mad, confused, excited or even bored—just by moving my face." Nexi can even wink.

Of course, Nexi does not really have feelings. It is programmed to show different emotions when certain things happen. For example, people do not like it when someone moves too close and "gets in their face." Nexi is programmed to notice when a hand gets in its face or a person crowds too closely. This program makes the robot seem like a person. Wave a hand in its face, and Nexi turns its head away, blinks its eyes, and looks upset.

Nexi and Real People

Nexi was social so it was programmed to imitate and learn from people. Breazeal wanted Nexi to be able to interact with ordinary people. She did not want robots that could only be used by scientists. She thought that emotional robots like Nexi would be easy for people to like. In the lab, everyone on the team liked Nexi. Its feelings looked real. The team members said it almost seemed alive. They liked to interact with Nexi. They tried to teach it things.

Breazeal wanted to know if ordinary people would like and teach Nexi, too. During 2009, Nexi was going to the Boston Museum of Science. Breazeal said the team wanted

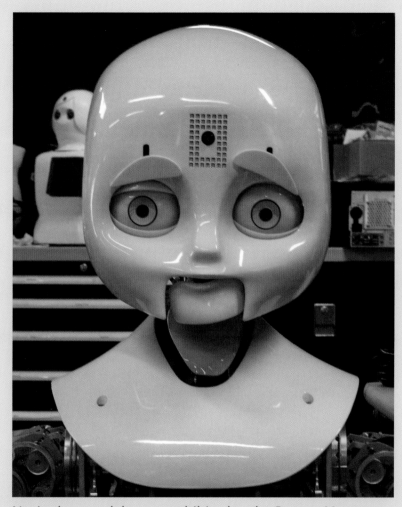

Nexi robot models were exhibited at the Boston Museum of Science in 2009. There, they interacted with visitors to the museum.

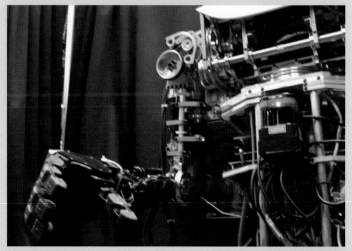

Nexi contains a complex computer and many technical robotic parts beneath its gentle exterior.

robots to get out of the lab and into the real world. She needed to know how regular people would try to teach robots. The team was building three more robots just like Nexi. The four Nexi robots would interact with visitors to the museum. On her MDS Research Web site, Breazeal said they would be in "a sort of robot Romper Room." In this playroom, people would try to teach the robots as if they were little children.

Nexi robots could not learn very much yet. They could not understand people's words. So visitors taught them something simple. They showed the robots how to stack blocks. Breazeal and her team studied how ordinary people taught Nexi robots. Breazeal did not yet know the different ways that people would use to try to teach Nexi. She did not know whether people would be patient when Nexi made mistakes. She hoped to find out what skills social robots needed to have in order to learn from regular people. Then the team would know what kind of learning abilities to program into a social robot.

May Nexi Help You?

Breazeal had another experiment at the museum, too. She wanted to know if people would take Nexi's advice. Nexi would serve people at a salad bar in the museum. It would ask them what ingredients they wanted. It would fill their plates. It would try to persuade them to make healthy choices. Would people take a robot's advice? Would they talk to the robot like a person? Breazeal did not know, but she wanted to find out. Since Nexi could not really hold a conversation, the team would use puppeteering to

Robot for Sale

Nexi may not be a perfect social robot, but Xitome is eager to sell Nexi robots. Xitome is the company that helped build Nexi's head and face. In October 2008 Xitome announced that robots based on Nexi were now for sale. Each robot will be built to order for each buyer, and costs vary. Some people estimate that it will cost as much as a luxury car.

make Nexi talk with people. Team members controlled what Nexi said with a remote computer. In the end, they hoped to learn enough to build future social robots even better than Nexi and even more likable.

Nexi was a wonderful social robot, but it was just a beginning for Breazeal. She and her team wanted to practice with Nexi and learn from it. Their goal was to build much more complex, teachable social robots. Only then would personal robots become a reality for ordinary people in everyday life.

Chapter 4

Partners for People

Someday, says Breazeal, everyone will be able to own a personal robot that is even better than Nexi. In a Science Week Lecture Series in Ireland in 2008, Breazeal gave a talk called "The Personal Side of Robots." She told the audience "the final frontier [for robots] is in your living room." She explained, "I think we're just at the threshold between the first personal robots we see today in terms of

Cynthia Breazeal speaks on robotics during an interview. Breazeal believes that humans will rely on and need robots in daily life in the near future.

toys and vacuum cleaners and so forth to what they could be in the years to come." In the future, robots will be personal because they will be social and emotional. They will be able to understand people and learn from them. They will communicate emotionally with people and respond correctly to emotions. People and robots will be able to work together. As this happens, robots become companions and partners for people. That is Breazeal's highest goal. She wants people to enjoy robots, and she predicts that personal robots will help people to live better, happier lives.

Robots for Hire

Social robots could help people in many ways. For example, a real social robot could do a lot of boring jobs that people do not enjoy. Perhaps it could be a waiter in a restaurant, like Nexi at the salad bar. It would understand and take orders from people, talk to them about what they wanted, and serve their meals. It would know whether customers were happy with their meals. It would know what to do if customers complained. It would understand if someone said, "Please reheat my mashed potatoes," or "Bring me a second piece of pie."

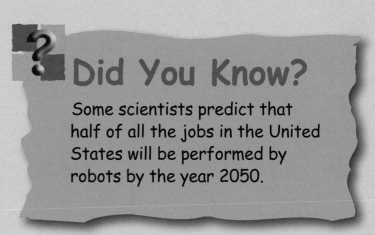

Did You Know?

Some scientists predict that half of all the jobs in the United States will be performed by robots by the year 2050.

Visitors at the Institute of Robotics in Germany enjoy the antics of Justin the robot. Social robots are designed to be pleasantly appealing to people.

Avoiding the Creep Factor

Robot scientists have discovered an important fact about people. People like robots that look a little bit human but not too much. When a robot looks too much like a human, it stops looking alive. Japanese roboticist Masahiro Mori studied this human response to robots. He called it the "uncanny valley." *Uncanny* means "weird" or "eerie." Mori explained that a robot face and body are uncanny when the robot is built to look almost human. Mori says that a robot face can be 99 percent human. But then people notice the 1 percent that is not human. Maybe its eyes do not sparkle with life. Perhaps it is a little too stiff when it moves. People see that it does not look exactly right. They feel disgusted. They think the robot is like a zombie. It makes people uncomfortable. That is why Nexi is designed to look like a cartoon character or a creature. It is designed to be cute so that people will not think the robot is creepy. Cynthia Breazeal believes that personal robots for people's homes should always look small and cute. People will enjoy them instead of thinking they are strange and different.

Roommate, Housekeeper, and Friend

Breazeal has another idea. She thinks about when she is old and retired from robotics work. In her lecture, she says, "I still want to cook my own meals. I still want to garden. I still want to do all the things that I do and enjoy in life. But I might want something to be able to help me." That something would be a friendly, small, and cute personal robot. It would have emotions and show its feelings, like Nexi. It would seem like a living creature. The robot could clean the house, take out trash, lift heavy things, and make Breazeal's life easy and comfortable.

A helper robot in the house would not be just a tool. It would know how to learn from its owner. The owner would teach it what to do. As the robot learned what the owner wanted, it would get smarter and more independent. For example, robots today can pick up drinking glasses and put them

Helper robots of the future will learn and remember their owners' habits, likes, and dislikes.

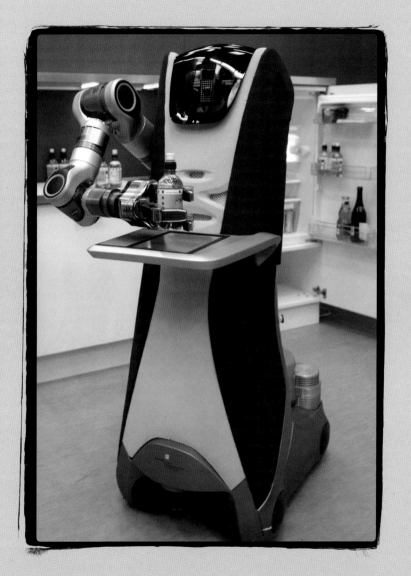

Did You Know?

In 2009 a computer science team at MIT developed gardening robots. These robots are growing cherry tomato plants in a laboratory farm. They water, fertilize, and harvest the ripe tomatoes without any human help.

on a shelf—over and over and over. A social robot would do much more. It could learn which shelf is for plates and which is for glasses. It could be taught to organize the glasses by size. It could be given another job when the last glass is put away. It could be told to go get a glass, fill it with water, and bring it to its owner. If the robot did not understand, it would show confusion on its face. The owner would understand the emotion. He or she would explain or show the robot what to do.

In time, the robot would learn how to get along in the home. It would learn the jobs that the owner needed it to do. It would grow in understanding, just as a small child does. Perhaps it would even learn how to garden if Breazeal wanted to give up that job. A true social robot could learn many different skills.

Robot Pets

Many elderly people are lonely and unable to care for themselves. Some live in nursing homes. Breazeal says that these people could be happier if they owned a

Pets like this Japanese robot kitten could provide good company for ill or lonely people who are unable to care for a real pet.

robot pet. It might be fluffy and furry. It might be like Huggable, only smart and social. It could have emotions, like a dog. People in nursing homes could hug the robot and interact with it. Maybe it would smile and laugh. Maybe it would like to be tickled or play a game of fetch. Maybe it would talk, or maybe it would make animal sounds. Whatever people like best, the robot pet could be programmed to do.

Even people in their own homes could enjoy a robot pet. These people might be too sick, too old, or too busy to care for a living pet. So a robot pet would be perfect. It would respond to the owner's emotions. It would have its own emotions and be like a friend. Breazeal explains in her Science Week lecture that complex social robots would not exactly have human emotions. They would have "robot emotions." She says dogs do not have human emotions either. "They're dog emotions," but people relate to and understand a dog's feelings. The same would be true for human-robot friendships. Robot pets would be different kinds of friends than dogs. She adds, "We don't know . . . what the human-robot relationship is really going to be." She does believe, however, that robot pets and friends will comfort people and make their lives better.

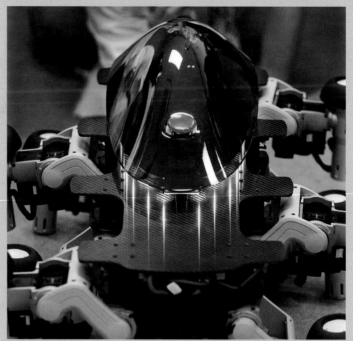

Robots of the future may take different forms, depending on their use. Japan's Halluc II, shown here, is built like a cockroach so it can travel anywhere and perhaps go on dangerous search-and-rescue missions someday.

Robots to the Rescue

Robot friends in nursing homes and hospitals could even be medical helpers. They could report to doctors about how patients are doing. They could take temperatures and blood pressure. They could give out medicines at the right time. They could get help if someone falls. They could sit with and listen to patients who are lonely or worried.

Breazeal thinks robots could do even more difficult jobs. She thinks that someday they could team up with people such as firefighters or rescue workers. The robots would do the most dangerous tasks so that people would not have to risk their own lives to save others. Breazeal imagines many, many uses for robot partners.

Nursemaids and Teachers

Kids almost always like robots. Social robots of the future might be babysitters for little children. They could play, tell stories, sing songs, and give hugs and kisses. They could guard small children from danger. Parents could teach the robot where the children are allowed to play and what they are allowed to do.

Children usually like robots, which may serve as babysitters or teachers' helpers in the future.

The Fashion Model

A Japanese robot named HRP-4C is built to be a fashion model. She has a silvery, metallic body and a face like a drawing in a Japanese comic book. She is 5 feet, 2 inches (158cm) tall and built to be beautiful. She is a fashion model in Tokyo. She can strike a model's poses, show off new clothing, and smile or pout with puppeteering through a remote computer. Her designers say that she is not built to help people. She is made to entertain people.

HRP-4C, the Japanese humanoid robot shown here, has a very lifelike face. The robot is used as a fashion model.

Older children might have robots for learning companions. They could read homework assignments together. Perhaps the robot could even do the teaching. It could explain math problems, for example. If the student was confused, the robot would understand his or her emotions. It would change its teaching style. It would not get impatient or irritated. It would work at the student's speed and make sure he or she learned. Robots might make school learning a lot of fun. Maybe robot and student could even complain about the teacher to each other!

Robots and People Together

Microsoft founder Bill Gates says that there will be a robot in every home by the year 2050. Some of these robots will be tools, but some will be social robots. Robotics experts such as Breazeal are working to make this idea a reality. In an interview for *Scholastic News,* she told Scholastic Kid Reporter Annie Vernick, "I dream of a future where robots are a **beneficial** part of everyday life for everyone—helping people, being companions for people, enriching our lives." Breazeal knows that it will be years before her social robots leave the lab and move into people's homes. But she thinks that her children will see that day when they are grown. Nexi is just the beginning. Breazeal does not know what her next robot project will be. Chances are, however, that her next robot will be even more social and skillful than Nexi. It will be another step toward a future of human-robot partners.

 **Glossary**

beneficial: Good and helpful.

conveyor belt: A continuously moving belt that carries packages or materials in a factory from one place to another.

dexterity/dexterous: Skill and cleverness in the use of the hands. Able to use the hands to explore the environment smoothly and skillfully. Using hands to handle, move, work, and control objects.

environment: Surroundings, including physical space and conditions, objects, and people.

imitating: Copying the actions or behavior of someone else.

innovative: New and creative; ahead of the times.

interact: Act together with or towards others; communicate or work together.

programmed: Given a set of instructions in computer language so as to perform a task.

puppeteering: Controlling an object as if it is a puppet on strings. In robotics, this means operating the robot by remote control through a computer. The robot is the puppet of the computer operator. The operator decides what the robot will do; it does not act independently based on a program.

robotics: The science and technology of designing, building, and operating robots.

social: Living with and pleasantly relating to other living beings as a cooperative member of a group.

 **For More Information**

Books

Toney Allman, *From Bug Legs to Walking Robots (Imitating Nature)*. Detroit: Kid-Haven Press, 2006. Scientists are using examples from nature to build robots that imitate the skills of insects. Discover robots built like cockroaches and spiders to explore their environments.

Roger Bridgman, *Robot*. DK Eyewitness Books. New York: DK Children, 2004. All kinds of robots appear in this book. There are insect robots, pet robots, robots that play games, robots that work, and robots that think.

Jordan D. Brown, *Robo World: The Story of Robot Designer Cynthia Breazeal*. Women's Adventures in Science. New York: Children's Press, 2005. Readers can follow Breazeal's life from a young girl interested in sports and science to her career as a roboticist at MIT. Details of her robot creations are also described.

Jennifer Fretland VanVoorst, *Rise of the Thinking Machines: The Science of Robots*. Headline: Science. Mankato, MN: Compass Point Books, 2008. Learn about the robots of today and the efforts to design artificial intelligence for robots of the future.

Steve D. White, *Military Robots*. New York: Children's Press/High Interest Books, 2007. Robots are changing the ways soldiers go into battle. They do dangerous jobs and protect soldiers' lives. Learn about the different kinds of robot warriors and how they operate in war zones.

Web Sites to Visit

**"Cynthia Breazeal: The Robot Designer,"
I Was Wondering . . .** (www.iwaswonder
ing.org/cynthia_homepage.html). This
site explores Breazeal's life and work and
describes her first social robot, Kismet.

**Tom Harris, "How Robots Work," How
StuffWorks.** (http://science.howstuff
works.com/robot.htm). This long article
covers what robots are, how they work,
different kinds of robots, and the artificial
intelligence necessary to build robots of
the future.

High Tech Robots—Kids Web Japan
(http://web-japan.org/kidsweb/hitech/
robot/index.html). Most people in Japan
love robots. At this site, visitors can see
some of the latest Japanese robotic inventions.

**Official MDS Robot Video—First Test
of Expressive Ability. YouTube** (www.
youtube.com/watch?v=aQS2zxmrrrA&
feature=related). This YouTube video
shows the first test of Nexi's ability to
express emotion at Breazeal's MIT lab.
Visitors can watch Nexi display emotions, hear it speak, and see how its body
works without the skin.

**Personal Robots Group—MIT Media
Lab** (http://robotic.media.mit.edu/index.
html). This is the home page for Cynthia
Breazeal's Personal Robots Group. Click
on Nexi's image to read about and see the
robot. Click the Projects link to access information about many of the latest robots
designed by the team.

**Weight Maintenance Sociable Robot—
The Media Lab** (www.media.mit.edu/?p=
114). In this video from MIT, Cory Kidd
explains Autom the weight-loss coach. He
demonstrates how Autom works and how
it was designed and built.

Index

About the Author

Toney Allman holds degrees from Ohio State University and the University of Hawaii. She currently lives in Virginia, where she enjoys writing nonfiction books for students while her vacuuming robot cleans the floors.